THE SKY'S THE LIMIT!

Canadians Who Blazed a Trail in Aviation

WANDA TAYLOR

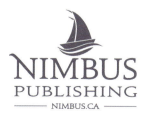

NIMBUS PUBLISHING
— NIMBUS.CA —

Text copyright © Wanda Taylor, 2025

All rights reserved. No part of this book may be reproduced, stored in a retrieval system or transmitted in any form or by any means without the prior written permission from the publisher, or, in the case of photocopying or other reprographic copying, permission from Access Copyright, 1 Yonge Street, Suite 1900, Toronto, Ontario M5E 1E5.

Nimbus Publishing Limited
3660 Strawberry Hill Street, Halifax, NS, B3K 5A9
(902) 455-4286 nimbus.ca

Printed and bound in Canada
NB1733

Design: Bee Stanton

Nimbus Publishing is based in Kjipuktuk, Mi'kma'ki, the traditional territory of the Mi'kmaq People.

No part of this book may be used in the training of generative artificial intelligence technologies or systems.

Library and Archives Canada Cataloguing in Publication
Title: The sky's the limit! : Canadians who blazed a trail in aviation / Wanda Taylor.
Names: Taylor, Wanda Lauren, author
Description: Includes bibliographical references and index.
Identifiers: Canadiana (print) 20240510534 | Canadiana (ebook) 20240510569 | ISBN 9781774712672 (softcover) | ISBN 9781774712863 (EPUB)
Subjects: LCSH: Air pilots—Canada—Biography—Juvenile literature. | LCSH: Aeronautics—Canada—History—Juvenile literature. | LCGFT: Biographies.
Classification: LCC TL547 .T39 2025 | DDC j629.13092/271—dc23

Nimbus Publishing acknowledges the financial support for its publishing activities from the Government of Canada, the Canada Council for the Arts, and from the Province of Nova Scotia. We are pleased to work in partnership with the Province of Nova Scotia to develop and promote our creative industries for the benefit of all Nova Scotians.

TABLE OF CONTENTS

Introduction — 4

1: Early Canadian Aviation & the RCAF — 11
2: Flying Pilot Allan Bundy — 25
3: Flying Officer Junius Lyman Edward Hokan — 35
4: Indigenous Flyers — 42
5: Women in Aviation — 56
6: A New Generation of Aviators — 67

Appendix A: Canada's Aviation Museums — 74
Appendix B: Flight Simulators — 78
Appendix C: How to Become a Pilot in Canada — 79

Glossary — 81
References — 84
Image Credits — 85
Index — 86

INTRODUCTION

Fasten your seat belts and get ready for an exciting ride in the skies! The life of a **pilot** can be amazing and fun. As you travel through these stories of Canadian aviators, you will encounter extraordinary people whose work involves soaring above the clouds. You will get to learn how some of their **aircraft** operate, as well as Canada's fascinating role in the history of **aviation**. You will be inspired by the possibility that you too can dream of a career in the sky.

There are many great sayings about the world above us, like *the sky's the limit* and *reach for the stars*. They encourage people to follow their dreams and to not be afraid to put in the work to make them come true. That means even more to those who dream of working in aviation and those who dream of becoming a pilot. But a career in aviation has not always been available to everyone.

For some communities, flying or working with planes in other ways was only a dream for a long time. Black people, Indigenous people, other people of colour, women, and people with disabilities were just some who faced obstacles. Yet there were a few exceptions who were determined to push through. We call them trailblazers. Some of them may have had fears, but they made their dream a reality. More importantly, their bravery helped to blaze a trail for the many aviators who came after them.

*Definitions for terms set in **bold** can be found in the glossary on page 81.*

TYPES OF PILOTS

When someone decides they want to be a pilot, there are a few ways they can make that happen. The route they take might depend on what kind of pilot they want to be. The three main types are private pilot, commercial pilot, and airline transport pilot. There are also military pilots, and they follow a different path because of their unique responsibility to the Canadian government.

A large commercial airplane.

A *private pilot* is someone who can carry only a few passengers, perhaps for recreation or to fly for business. They can also buy their own small plane and fly it. A private pilot is not allowed to fly a commercial plane.

A *commercial pilot* can carry many passengers and may also carry animals. They can work as a pilot for an airline as part of a crew. That crew would include a co-pilot and flight attendants. Commercial pilots can also fly smaller planes.

An *air transport pilot* flies as a captain for air transport operations. They can carry anything from passengers for domestic and international flights, to goods ready for exporting.

Beginners will usually learn to fly in either a Piper Archer or a Cessna. These are both single-engine planes,

THE PIPER ARCHER VERSUS THE CESSNA 172

Most pilots train on one of these two planes. How do they compare?

The **Piper Archer**, also known as the PA-28, has higher visibility. This allows for passengers to get a better view of the scenery below. This plane is also better for taking off in a shorter field. One of its downsides is its design. There is only one door and you have to climb on a wing in order to get inside.

Cessna 172 (left), Piper Archer (right).

The **Cessna 172**, on the other hand, has two doors, two windows, and air vents overhead. The two doors make entry easier, and there is more space inside. The windows and vents provide more air circulation. The Cessna's wings also act as a shelter from rain. This plane is also better for carrying heavy loads.

Both planes have good speed and are equally safe. They both do their jobs well—and they are both a lot of fun!

which means they only need one engine to fly. (There are other planes that have up to four engines, like the 747 jet airliner!)

BECOMING A MILITARY PILOT IN CANADA

A *military pilot*, one who works for the Canadian government, follows a slightly different path. In order to become a pilot in the Royal Canadian Air Force (RCAF), one has to complete basic military training and military officer qualification training.

The Sky's the Limit!

CAN PILOTS BE DEAF?

Yes! People who are Deaf can also learn to fly. If they achieve a pilot's license, their certificate will say "Not Valid for Flights Requiring the Use of Radio." That is because Deaf pilots are restricted in their ability to hear radio frequencies. This limitation is meant to keep these pilots and others in the air safe.

The RCAF is one of three branches of the Canadian military known as the Canadian Armed Forces (CAF). The **Air Force**'s role is to protect and defend the airspace in Canada from any threats or harm. That could be from an enemy attack or any other outside force. The RCAF is also a part of the North Atlantic Treaty Organization (NATO) whose mission is to protect member nations for international peace and security.

A person must be at least sixteen years old to enrol in the RCAF. First, they attend the Canadian Forces Leadership and Recruit School in Quebec. This is where they will complete their twelve-week basic military training. During that time, recruits learn about the work of the military, the RCAF, leadership skills, first aid, and how to handle weapons. They also participate in physical training exercises, so they need to be healthy and fit. In order to move on to additional training, they must complete basic training successfully. Then they will have all the skills they need to be a part of Canada's military.

Next, recruits take Primary Flying Training at the Canadian Forces Flying Training School in Manitoba, then Basic Flying Training at the NATO Flight Training Centre

Introduction

Canadian Military Pilot Wings.

in Moose Jaw, Saskatchewan. Based on their performance, the pilots will be placed on one of three paths: *Rotary Wing Training*, where they will take a **helicopter** course flying the CH-139 Jet Ranger or the Airbus H135 helicopter; *Multi-Engine Training*, where they train on the King Air C-90B; or *Fast Jet*, where they train as a fighter pilot and an instructor pilot on the CT-156 Harvard II.

Once military pilots complete their advanced training, they receive a badge to wear called pilot wings. After final operational training in an aircraft, they are assigned to a squadron, which is their team of military aircrew and aircraft.

The **CH-139 Jet Ranger** is a single-engine trainer. It is one of the helicopters the RCAF uses for trainees to earn their wings. The pilot seats are side-by-side and each one includes flight controls for both the pilot and for the trainer.

BUSY PILOTS

Every type of pilot has a busy life. Some fly all over the world. They can fly at any time of day or night. Military pilots are often tasked with training for missions. They may also be involved in search-and-rescue operations, transporting, and patrolling. A commercial pilot may land

The Sky's the Limit!

When pilots are selected for the multi-engine stream, they will train using the **C-90B King Air**. And after learning how to fly with a crew in this plane, then can receive their wings.

Because of its great performance and handling, and the advanced layout of the cockpit, the **CT-156 Harvard II** is used to help pilots transition from basic training to jet training.

in South America one week and take off from Canada the next. They can also have a job where they are gone for many days at a time, with many **stopovers**. If a pilot only works in a certain location or region, they may land in that area many times during the course of one day. Helicopter pilots tend to make shorter trips, and can make more than fifteen to twenty landings and takeoffs in one day!

When commercial pilots arrive for their shift, they must perform certain duties before they take off. That might include inspecting the plane or getting up-to-date information on the weather. Inside the plane, they will make sure their navigation computers are loaded. Their job is not only to fly the plane, but to get their passengers or goods to their destinations safely. Pilots take that responsibility seriously. They are doing what they love, while providing a service to others. This goes for all pilots, including military pilots. They serve the country, and they work to keep the country safe.

Introduction

LIFE ABOVE THE CLOUDS

The job of a pilot can be quite busy, but it can also be very rewarding. Sometimes there is **turbulence** in the sky, when the plane feels like it's rolling over bumps and potholes. That can seem scary, but pilots are trained to navigate through it. And when there is no turbulence, the skies are open and welcoming. It's amazing to be a passenger and look out the window. You can see the clouds beneath you, and the sky stretching out right in front of you.

When you fly in a plane as a passenger, it's easy to see why pilots love their work. The sky is their office. When you are above the clouds, you are on top of the world, and everything feels peaceful, calm, and serene.

We are thankful to the first aviators who made a career in the skies. In this book, you will meet aviators who played important roles in the Royal Canadian Air Force, like Black pilots Allan Bundy and Junius Hokan, and Indigenous pilots like Gwich'in pilot Fred Carmichael and Cree pilot Kimberly Ballantyne. They soared so others could too. You will learn about other amazing flyers who overcame obstacles to fulfill their dreams. Many of them are still working as pilots and might be flying above you as you read this book.

Maybe some of these flying trailblazers will inspire you to dream of a career in the sky!

1: EARLY CANADIAN AVIATION & THE RCAF

WHAT IS THE ROYAL CANADIAN AIR FORCE?

The story of the Royal Canadian Air Force (RCAF) goes way back to the beginning of Canada's experiments with aviation in the early 1900s. After much trial and error, these experiments showed that aviation could actually serve a greater purpose, and Canada began using aircraft during the First World War.

First, Canada formed the Canadian Aviation Corps (CAC), but it didn't see any action. Canadian pilots flew in the First World War with either the British Royal Flying Corps (RFC) or the British Royal Naval Air Service (RNAS). Billy Bishop, for example, flew with the RFC.

The Royal Canadian Air Force, formed in 1924, it eventually became the air and space military of Canada. It remains a valuable part of the country's national defence. Among many other duties, the RCAF provides air power to the Canadian Armed Forces, with their fleet of aircraft.

There are over a hundred different kinds of jobs in the Royal Canadian Air Force! That includes everything from **aerospace** control officer and medical technician, to military police officer, to fighter pilot. There are so many amazing opportunities and incredible ways to contribute to the field of aviation. But just like pilots follow a path to a career in aviation, the RCAF also followed a path to becoming what it is today. To understand what some of Canada's trailblazing pilots went through to fly, we need to know more about the RCAF's path, too.

BEFORE THE RCAF

At the very beginning of the First World War, which happened between 1914 and 1918, Canada did not really have much air defence. But after seeing that countries in Europe were using aircraft, Canada created a very small unit they called the Canadian Aviation Corps (CAC). The Corps was made up of just two officers and one mechanic! They received five thousand dollars to buy and ship a Burgess-Dunne floatplane over to England. But by 1915, the Corps had still not fought in battle and was disbanded. Then, in 1916, the British Royal Flying Corps set up schools in Canada to train pilots.

Two amazing pilots who graduated and became Canadian **aces** were Billy Bishop and William Barker. Altogether, over 22,000 Canadians served with the British air services in the First World War. After they were dismissed from their service, Canadian troops were sent home and a small flying program was

Canada's first military aircraft was the Burgess-Dunne floatplane.

CANADA'S FIRST FLYERS

In the summer of 1885, Alexander Graham Bell visited Baddeck in Cape Breton, Nova Scotia, from Washington, DC, where he lived with his wife and two daughters. Everyone in Cape Breton knew who he was, because he had invented the telephone. He said Cape Breton's countryside reminded him of his hometown in Scotland.

One day, Bell saw a man in the *Cape Breton Island Reporter* newspaper office struggling with his telephone. Bell offered to help, and took the phone apart. He pulled out a dead fly and the phone worked again. The man he helped was Arthur McCurdy, and they became friends. And Arthur's son John Alexander Douglas McCurdy became the pilot who completed the very first flight in Canada.

Flight of the Silver Dart aircraft over the Bras d'Or Lakes, Cape Breton, NS, 1909.

John studied at the School of Mechanical Engineering at the University of Toronto, then returned to Baddeck. He and several other engineers started a group with Alexander Graham Bell called the Aerial Experiment Association. Their goal was to get a man up in the air.

The first of the four aeroplanes built by the Aerial Experiment Association was called the **Red Wing**. It crashed on its second flight because the pilot, Casey Baldwin, lost control. The Association worked to try and fix the instability in their aircraft and invented moveable wing tips, which they put into their second aircraft, the **White Wing**. The third aircraft was called the **June Bug** and the fourth was the *Silver Dart*.

John flew the *Silver Dart* in Baddeck in the winter of 1909, and he became the first person to successfully fly a plane in the collection of countries we now call the British Commonwealth. He made Canadian flying history!

Chapter 1: Early Canadian Aviation & the RCAF

eventually established in 1920, called the Canadian Air Force. It consisted mainly of pilots who had returned from war.

FACING OBSTACLES TO ENLISTING

While a career in the air was a wonderful reality to many, for others it could only be a dream. When the First World War began in 1914, people who weren't from Europe or didn't have parents or other ancestors from Europe had trouble joining the military, which was called *enlisting*. It is estimated that over four thousand Indigenous men volunteered for overseas service in the First World War. However, historians have said that thousands of these men did not say they were Indigenous when they filled out their **recruitment** forms because they knew they wouldn't be allowed to enlist if the military knew they were Indigenous.

THE FIRST WORLD WAR AND THE BLACK BATTALION

The First World War started in 1914 when Germany invaded Belgium. When Britain, an ally of Belgium, joined in the fight against Germany, all of the countries that were part of the British Empire also had to go war. That included Canada.

Before the First World War, Canada's military was small, but when the war started and Canada had to help, over 650,000 Canadians rushed to join. But not all of them were welcomed.

The Sky's the Limit!

First World War veterans in London, England. Front row centre: Private John Alexander Paris, No. 2 Construction Battalion.

Black people who tried to enlist were turned away. They were told that it was a "white man's war." It wasn't just the recruitment officers who were racist; many white soldiers said they would never fight alongside Black people. Community leaders wrote to the government complaining about the unfair practices against Black people. They said it was unacceptable and they wanted change.

By 1916, Canada was in desperate need of military labour units—people who would build roads, bridges, and trenches (long, deep holes dug through the ground to protect soldiers from enemy attacks)—to help support the fighting troops.

Britain sent a request to Canada to form two labour **battalions**. Canada then decided that one of those battalions could be made up of Black people, but that they would not be allowed to fight on the front lines in battle, like the other labour battalion did. The Eastern Ontario Regiment were all skilled labourers. But by February 1915, they were deep in the trenches.

No. 2 Battalion recruitment poster.

By July 1916, the No. 2 Construction Battalion was formed and the military began enlisting men from across

Chapter 1: Early Canadian Aviation & the RCAF

the Maritime provinces. On March 28, 1917, the battalion was sent to England from Halifax and was eventually sent to France to support the Canadian Forestry Corps. They built a logging road and cut trees to transport to the mills for sawing. The lumber was needed in the trenches on the front lines for building things like the barracks where soldiers slept, and the mess halls where they ate. Their work doubled how much lumber the mills could make, but these Black soldiers lived in separate camps, without access to the same food and medical supplies as the white soldiers.

This stamp was created in 2016 to celebrate the commitment and efforts of the Black Battalion.

The No. 2 Construction Battalion was disbanded after the war. To this day, it is still the only all-Black unit in Canada's history, and for that reason it is also known as the *Black Battalion*. Almost no Canadian knew who they were or what they did until 1987, when Senator Calvin Ruck wrote the book *The Black Battalion, 1916–1920: Canada's Best Kept Military Secret*. Many African Nova Scotians in the military credit the soldiers of the Black Battalion with paving the way for them to also serve their country.

In 1993, a monument was erected in Pictou, Nova Scotia, to honor the Battalion for its service and contributions during the war. In 2022, the government finally made a

GEORGE BORDEN

After graduating high school, George Borden enlisted in the military with his two older brothers. Because he was only seventeen, he had to get permission from his parents. George served from 1953 to 1985. He was passionate about bringing greater recognition to the work of the Black Battalion, and worked tirelessly to demand a formal apology from the Government of Canada for the racism and discrimination experienced by the troops. That apology finally came in 2022 during a ceremony recognizing the bravery, efforts, and incredible service of the Black Battalion.

George Borden (centre) with his older brothers, Wilfred and Curtiss.

Borden and his sister Ozell with the Legacy Shadow Quilt commemorating the 100th anniversary of the Battalion.

public apology about the treatment of the troops. It made a commitment to address racism in the military and take steps to tackle it in the future. George Borden and others were also thanked for their years of work demanding recognition for the Battalion soldiers.

The Black Cultural Centre for Nova Scotia has served as a major voice for bringing awareness to new generations about the Black Battalion soldiers. Each year the centre holds a remembrance ceremony to ensure the Black Battalion is never forgotten.

THE SECOND WORLD WAR

The 7th Brigade moves through a village near Leopold canal in Belgium during the Second World War, October 18, 1944.

The Second World War was the largest war in history. It involved over thirty countries. This terrible war made it clear how important aviation was for Canada and its military, and it also provided opportunities for people of colour to contribute to the war efforts.

The war started in Europe when Nazi Germany invaded Poland in September 1939. Germany was being ruled by Adolph Hitler, and he wanted to rule all of Europe. Following the invasion of Poland, Britain and France declared war on Germany. Canada had to fight on Britain's side again.

Many Canadians, both men and women, signed up for the military to help in the war. But as the nasty conflict raged on, Canada lost a lot of soldiers, and there were not enough qualified people available to serve. The military realized it had to change its rules. It began recruiting many people who were previously shut out, and many Black and Indigenous men answered the call.

That included the five Carty Brothers. The siblings were originally from Sackville, New Brunswick. Their father, Albert Carty, had served in the No. 2 Construction Battalion

The Carty Brothers. (L–R): Adolphus, William, Clyde, Donald, and Gerald

during the First World War. The oldest brothers, Adolphus and William, enlisted in September 1939. The other three, Clyde, Donald, and Gerald, enlisted in 1942.

All five of the Carty brothers served Canada during the Second World War. Flight Sergeant Adolphus Carty was a skilled airframe mechanic. Flight Sergeant William Carty was an aeronautical inspector. Aircraftman (Second Class) Donald Carty was an equipment assistant. And Leading Aircraftman Clyde Carty was a firefighter. To round out the five, their younger brother, Gerald Carty, enlisted at age eighteen and became one of the youngest commissioned officers in the RCAF.

Indigenous members Combat Pilot Jack Beaver and Officer Willard John Bolduc both served in the RCAF from 1942 to 1943.

The recruiting policies of the RCAF were officially changed in March 1942, making way for many other diverse Canadians to also serve.

The **CF-188 Hornet**, also called the CF-18, is a powerful fighter aircraft, used for air defence, ground attacks, pilot training, demonstrations, and testing and evaluation. The Hornet is very fast, with a top speed of around 1,915 kilometres per hour at high altitudes. It is also capable of tracking targets. All of these great qualities make the Hornet a much-desired aircraft and has led to many military operation successes around the world.

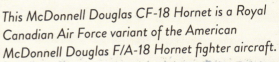

This McDonnell Douglas CF-18 Hornet is a Royal Canadian Air Force variant of the American McDonnell Douglas F/A-18 Hornet fighter aircraft.

THE CREATION OF THE RCAF

As part of the flying program established in 1920, pilots who returned from the First World War undertook some refresher training on a part-time basis. The Air Board for this flying program also oversaw aviation training for civilians and was in charge of the duties of the early Canadian Air Force in Europe. In 1921, Canada followed Australia by adding "Royal" to the Canadian Air Force title, though the name wasn't official until April 1, 1924. Aviation for the military really took off in 1924, after the Royal Canadian Air Force was officially formed.

On December 17, 1939, the Royal Canadian Air Force signed a training agreement for a British Commonwealth Air Training Plan. They agreed to train thousands of air crew and build new airfields and schools, setting up

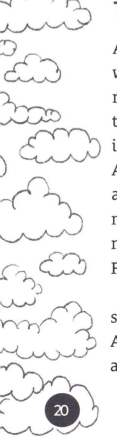

training at over 231 locations across Canada.

Today, various aircraft that pilots trained on during that time can be seen at the Commonwealth Air Training Plan Museum in Brandon, Manitoba. It would be great to compare the structures and engines of those earlier planes to aircraft that came later, like the CF-18 Hornet, which can be viewed in various military museums across the country.

In times leading up to the Second World War, Britain saw Canada's fighter squadrons as a support to their defences, in case Britain was attacked. By 1940, after the war had begun, the very first organized unit was trained and ready for travel overseas. The Royal Canadian Air Force began using its fighters in more offensive operations as well as defensive.

Because Canada had units in Britain, they also needed to have headquarters there. On January 1, 1940, an RCAF headquarters was established in England, and the next month the No. 110 Squadron left Canada for the United Kingdom. Between 1939 and 1945, over 232,000 men were enlisted with the Royal Canadian Air Force, as well as 17,000 women.

Sergeant MacKenzie of the RCAF Women's Division in the Motor Transport Section of RCAF Station Rockcliffe, Ontario, Canada. June 23, 1944.

Chapter 1: Early Canadian Aviation & the RCAF

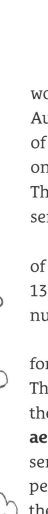

The RCAF was the first military in Canada to recruit women. On July 2, 1941, it formed the Canadian Women's Auxiliary Air Force. It later became the Women's Division of the Air Force. Wilhelmina Walker, also called Willa, was one of the highest-ranking RCAF women during that time. Thousands of other Canadian women volunteered their services.

After the war, there were about 18,000 active members of the air force. The Air Cadet League of Canada also had 135 squadrons, adding over 10,000 young cadets to that number.

One of the aircraft that served as the primary jet trainer for the Royal Canadian Air Force was the CT-114 Tutor. These planes are now mostly flown during public events by the Canadian Forces Snowbirds team. They are the military **aerobatics** flight demonstration team of the RCAF and serve as ambassadors to the Canadian Air Force as they perform across North America. They are respected around the world for their incredible feats of formation flying—it's almost like they're dancing together in the sky. The planes used by the Snowbirds have been modified so their

THE AIR CADET LEAGUE OF CANADA

The Air Cadet League of Canada was established in 1941 to train and prepare youth from ages twelve to eighteen for a potential career in aviation. Youth learn valuable skills such as leadership and good citizenship. Cadets participate in drills, learn survival and navigation skills, and study the principals of flight. Any Canadian youth twelve and older can register to join. It could be your first step toward a career in aviation!

demonstrations are more impressive. They have a highly tuned engine, a smoke generating system, and unique painted designs that identify the flying team.

Canadian Forces Snowbirds fly together during an air show in Niagara Falls, Ontario, 2018.

The flyers of these planes perform at events across Canada and the United States. To fly these aircraft in formation takes an incredible amount of teamwork. The Canadian Armed Forces requires pilots to be highly skilled, completely dedicated, and incredibly disciplined to successfully perform shows in the air.

RCAF TODAY

The Royal Canadian Air Force is in charge of all aircraft operations for the Canadian Armed Forces. As part of National Defence, the RCAF protects and secures Canada's airspace in many ways, including identifying foreign aircraft and providing air traffic services.

The RCAF also supplies aircraft to help the navy and army carry out their missions and works in partnership with the United States Air Force to help protect North America's airspace.

The National Search and Rescue Program of Canada relies on the Royal Canadian Air Force to supply resources in the air for their rescue missions. One of the commonly used aircraft is the CC-130H Hercules. It also carries out transport missions, but its main purpose is as a support for saving lives.

The CC-130H Hercules of the Royal Canadian Air Force is largely used for rescue missions.

The CC-130H Hercules can fly for 7,200 kilometres without stopping for fuel and it can carry up to eighty people at a time. It can also take off and land on short runways and fly in bad weather. All of that means the Hercules is a perfect aircraft for travelling over our huge country in all kinds of locations and conditions. It also makes this aircraft one of the best RCAF aircraft to support carrying out the important work of rescuing and saving lives.

Helicopters are also commonly used. Most squadrons are equipped with helicopters and fixed-wing aircraft. It's an important part of Canadian flight history—and its future too!

Badge of the Royal Canadian Air Force.

The Sky's the Limit!

2: FLYING PILOT ALLAN BUNDY

At the age of twenty-two, Allan Selwyn Bundy became one of the first two Black Canadian pilots in Canada, and the first Canadian-born Black combat pilot to serve in the RCAF during the Second World War. He broke racial barriers and paved the way for other pilots of colour. But the road toward fulfilling his dream of flying was not easy.

Allan Selwyn Bundy in his Royal Canadian Air Force uniform (left) and in civilian clothing (right).

Allan and his younger siblings, Carl, Milton, and Lillian, were born in Dartmouth, Nova Scotia, to First World War veteran Private William Bundy and his wife, Ruth. In 1916, at thirty-one years old, William had joined the Royal Engineers and served in France as a private in the No. 2 Construction Battalion. After the war, he moved to Dartmouth and became a firefighter for the Department of National Defence. He also met his wife.

ALLAN BUNDY'S DREAM

William and Ruth's son Allan was born in Dartmouth, too, in 1920. Allan had very early dreams of flying. Growing up, he and his brother excelled at sports. Allan was a pole vaulter and track-and-field runner at Dartmouth High. He was also gifted in school, and earned a scholarship from the Imperial Order of the Daughters of the Empire, a national women's charity. That scholarship paid for Allan to attend Dalhousie University, where he studied chemistry with the goal of becoming a doctor.

When the war broke out, Allan and his friend "Soupy" Campbell, who was white, wanted to serve their country. In 1940, at age nineteen, they decided to enlist in the Royal Canadian Air Force together. However, the RCAF still had policies that prevented Asian and Black people from enlisting. Soupy was immediately accepted into service, but Allan was rejected. Being turned away a crushing blow.

A CHANCE TO ENLIST

After two years at Dalhousie, Allan left university and went to work as with the Canadian National Railway. On January 13, 1942, he married Marie Della Kane. Then shortly after, Allan received a **conscription** notice, meaning the Canadian government was forcing him to join the army. But he ignored the **draft** on purpose. He thought back to 1940, and how he was turned away the first time he tried to serve his country. Why should he have to serve now, after being treated so badly just two years earlier? But this far into the war and with so many losses overseas, the armed forces in Canada were desperate for new recruits. They were forcing people to join.

Because Allan ignored the notice, the RCMP showed up at his door to enforce the draft order. Allan told them about his experience and questioned why he should join. The officer did not arrest Allan. Instead, he talked with him and gave him the chance to apply again.

SLEEPING CAR PORTERS

Porters were railway workers who took care of passengers aboard sleeping cars on trains. They carried luggage, made beds, served food, and shined shoes, among other things. Most were Black. A porter was one of the few jobs Black men in Canada could get in the early twentieth century. They worked long hours for very little pay and dealt with racism daily. In 1917, Black Canadian porters formed the very first Black railway union in North America.

Albert Budd, CPR, SC porter, 1940s–1960s.

After speaking with the RCMP officer that day, Allan decided to reapply. On June 17, 1942, two months after the Canadian military lifted the racial barriers to serving, Allan enlisted. His dream of becoming a pilot was finally closer than ever.

Chapter 2: Flying Pilot Allan Bundy

Pilot Officer Tarrance Freeman (lower right), a navigator from Windsor, sits with his bomber crew.

MANY FIRSTS

Pilot Officer Tarrance Freeman of Windsor, Ontario, was the first Black pilot to be commissioned, or hired, in the RCAF, on July 9, 1943. He attended Patterson Collegiate and the Windsor Vocational School before the RCAF, and did his flight training in London, Ontario. He is believed to be the first Black Canadian **navigator** in the RCAF.

Tarrance was not quite the first Black Canadian in the RCAF—E. V. Watts and Gerald Bell joined before him. And the first Black Canadian combat pilot was Allan Bundy. Still, Tarrance's accomplishments are notable and important.

TRAINING BEGINS

Two months later, Allan started his training in Quebec, then went on to complete training in Ontario. Allan performed smaller jobs, like cleaning planes, while waiting for a spot in the pilot training course to open up. He eventually trained on the basics of aviation, then went on to pilot training. On December 30, 1942, he graduated from the No. 1 Initial Training School in Toronto, becoming Leading Aircraftman Bundy.

By May 1943, Allan was in Aylmer, Ontario, training at the No. 14 Service Flying Training School. There he learned military flying and the twin-engine aircraft. When he graduated with high standing in September 1943, he was awarded the Royal Canadian Air Force pilot wings and was commissioned as a Pilot Officer, what would today be called Second Lieutenant. News outlets in Canada and the US posted stories about Allan's commission. In an article written about him in the *Toronto Star*, Allan said he had every expectation to continue his studies and become a doctor. But added, if all went well with flying, he would give up that idea. By all accounts, his career as a pilot was exceptional, and Allan never returned to his medical studies.

A NEAR TRAGEDY

During his RCAF training, Allan was in an accident that could have killed him. The *Pittsburgh Courier*, a top African American newspaper in the US that followed Allan's career, wrote that while Allan was posted to No. 7 Elementary Flying Training School in Windsor, Ontario, his aircraft stalled at 250 feet during a solo flight, and it crashed to the ground. The newspaper reported, "He catapulted headfirst through the fabric covering of the cockpit."

Allan was hospitalized for a month while being treated for his injuries, which included a fractured skull. Allan later told one reporter, "At first they thought I was going to die… but I got completely better."

Despite that setback, Allan pressed on with his dream. When he was healed, he continued the work and went on to graduate to the next phase of his training.

THE OVERSEAS MISSIONS

By the end of 1943, Allan was posted overseas in the UK. He had become highly skilled in flying the Bristol Beaufighter and was ready to be assigned to a fighting squadron. The Beaufighter is a two-person aircraft, where the pilot and navigator must perform as a team. However, Allan was informed that no one would agree to fly with him as his navigator. No one wanted to fly with a Black pilot. Allan had no choice but to transfer to a fighter squadron, which was not what he wanted. But while he was awaiting the transfer, Flight Sergeant Harry Elwood Wright stepped up and volunteered to be Allan's partner.

Flight Sergeant Wright was a pilot who showed great leadership. He was awarded the Distinguished Flying Cross and Bar and the Distinguished Flying Medal for a night attack on Modane, France, in 1943, and for his consistently high standards of leadership and courage.

Volunteering to be Allan's partner despite the racism of the times was a true demonstration of that leadership.

Flying Officer Allan Bundy and Flight Sergeant Elwood Wright were then posted at 404 (The Buffalo Squadron)

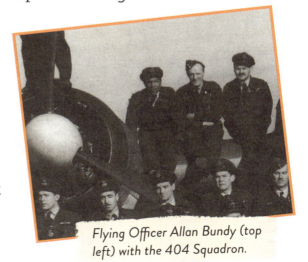

Flying Officer Allan Bundy (top left) with the 404 Squadron.

The Sky's the Limit!

A close-up of the Bristol Beaufighter.

operating from Royal Air Force base Dallachy in Scotland. The role of the 404 squadron was to make sure enemy ships that were not supposed to be there were kept away. To accomplish this, they attacked ships off the Norwegian coast. A lot of fighting during the war took place on the water and along the coast of Norway.

The squadron was also tasked with carrying out armed inspections of territory from the air and conducting anti-submarine patrols. They had the job of protecting Scotland's coasts as well by sinking enemy ships as they arrived from occupied Norway and disrupting German shipping moving along the coasts. Their Bristol Beaufighter was heavily armed with cannons and rocket projectiles.

Their first mission took place in October 1944. The squadron sent twelve aircraft to add to their larger formation in order to launch an attack on a tanker and a German warship. The squadron sank both of them, with the help of Allan's skill in firing his rockets at the tanker.

Large formations like this included fighter protection so military could defend themselves against German air attacks. They also included **anti-flak** aircraft to keep heavy defensive fire at bay, other rocket-carrying aircraft such as torpedoes, and a search-and-rescue

The De Havilland Mosquito, nicknamed "Mossie."

plane that could send a lifeboat if any crew was shot down.

That search-and-rescue aircraft was certainly needed on February 9, 1945, when six of 404 Squadron's Beaufighters were shot down. The event was called *Black Friday* by the surviving flyers. Two of the survivors were pilot Roger "Roj" Savard and Canadian airman Herbert "Bert" Ramsden.

Allan and his partner went on to fly forty-three more missions together before the war ended. Then, in April 1945, Allan's Squadron stopped flying Beaufighters and switched to the De Havilland Mosquito. It took Allan and his partner, Sergeant Wright, about three weeks to learn how to fly the new plane. After that, the partners were only able to complete two more missions, one in the middle of May. They were part of the naval force who had the job of flying some very important people to Norway. The second mission came shortly after. They had to fly along the Norwegian coast to provide reports on weather conditions.

The 404 Squadron was disbanded on May 25, 1945. Allan was returned to Canada, and he retired from service in August 1945, just before the war ended.

A DREAM DEFERRED

Allan came from a family of people committed to serving their country. Not only had his father served with the No. 2 Construction Battalion during the First World War, but his brother Carl also joined the RCAF in 1943. His youngest brother, Milton, had dreams of following in his father and brothers' footsteps by serving in the military, but was too young. In the meantime, he became a member of the No. 18 Royal Canadian Air Cadet Squadron in Dartmouth.

Allan Bundy in his Royal Canadian Air Force uniform.

Five years after Allan returned home from the war, tragedy struck his family, and the entire community. On November 30, 1950, Allan's father, William, fifty-one, and his brother Milton, twenty-one, were killed in a deadly fire at Kay's Department Store. Allan was devastated by this event, and saddened that his brother would not get to live out his dream.

MOVING ON

After this tragic loss, Allan and his wife moved to Toronto, Ontario, where Allan worked as a manufacturing supervisor.

Chapter 2: Flying Pilot Allan Bundy

THE ROYAL CANADIAN LEGION

The Royal Canadian Legion is a non-profit organization for military veterans across Canada. It also serves veteran police officers and air, army, and sea cadets. The legion first began in 1925 as a way to give voice to veterans who fought in the First World War. Following the Second World War, the needs of veterans increased and the Legion expanded its services. Originally it was formed under the name Dominion Veterans Alliance, and then it was called The Canadian Legion of the British Empire Service League. On December 19, 1960, the organization became The Royal Canadian Legion and continues to honour veterans across the country.

He became an active member of the Baron Byng Branch of the Royal Canadian Legion.

Later in life, Allan became sick. He kept a low profile and eventually stopped going to parties and club events. He died on December 9, 2001, after battling a long illness. However, his legacy and the trail he blazed for the pilots who came after him live on.

3: FLYING OFFICER JUNIUS LYMAN EDWARD HOKAN

Like Allan Bundy, Pilot Officer Junius Hokan blazed a trail as one of the first pilots of colour to fly with the Royal Canadian Air Force. Today he is still considered one of the most extraordinary Black Canadian pilots to touch the sky.

Junius was born in St. Catharines, Ontario, on March 4, 1922. He was an only child. His mother, Ella Grace Bollen, was a West Indian woman from Guelph, Ontario. His father, Kauri Lyman Hokan, was born in Hawaii, and eventually became a Canadian citizen. His father had enlisted in the Canadian Field Artillery in 1914 and served with the 14th Battery, 4th Brigade. He then arrived in France in 1915 and served with the Canadian Corps until 1919.

Junius was an excellent student. After he finished school, he attended St. Catharines Collegiate Institute and Vocational School. He excelled in drafting and studied **aerodynamics**. In 1939, he graduated with honours and got a job working as a draftsman. These were people with technical drawing skills. Nowadays, they are called engineering techs.

Pilot Officer Junius Hokan.

In 1940, Junius followed in his father's footsteps and enlisted to serve his country. He signed up in Niagara Falls,

Ontario, when he was just eighteen years old. People of colour were being turned away from enlisting during that time, but Junius was accepted. His skin colour was very fair, which may have been a factor. A comment written on his enlistment assessment stated: *Fine type of lad if no objection to ancestry.*

FROM TRAINING TO SERVICE

Junius started out with the No. 1 Initial Training School as Aircraftman Class 2, and learned the basics of flying. Then he attended training at No. 9 Elementary Flying Training School in St. Catharines. Once Junius completed his initial pilot training, he went on to the No. 2 Service Flying Training School at Uplands in Ottawa. There, he completed his advanced pilot training.

From left: Pilot Officer Junius Lyman Edward Hokan, Sergeant S. C. Creagh (Royal Australian Air Force), Sergeant K. Edwards (RAF), and Sergeant H. Fallon (RAF) pose with a Spitfire Mk Vb from 610 Squadron.

Junius received his pilot wings on August 8, 1941, and was commissioned as a pilot officer. Two weeks later, Pilot Officer Junius Hokan prepared to go to the UK. Upon arrival, he was transferred to the RAF at No. 3 Personnel Reception Centre. At the time, there was no squadron with space to take him, so Junius was sent to No. 56 Operational Training Unit. There he spent time learning the newest air combat techniques. Finally, in February 1942, Junius got posted to No. 610 Squadron. This was an RAF support squadron that fought during the Battle of Britain, when a small group of pilots claimed victory over the German air force.

When Junius was posted there, the squadron had been flying the Spitfire Mk Vb from the RAF station Hutton Cranswick. They were involved in intruder operations. Then after April 1942, they served as convoy protection, escorting or protecting large groups of ocean-going vessels (convoys) from enemy fire. When Squadron Leader J. E. "Johnnie" Johnson took over the squadron in August 1942, they had become an international unit with servicemen

Fourteen squadrons of the Royal Canadian Air Force flew the **Spitfire**. It also served in battle and was supplied to nine other countries around the world.

Supermarine Spitfire Mk Vb.

from many parts of the world, including France, Norway, and Australia.

Pilot Officer Junius was a highly skilled pilot. He was flying with another pilot when they shot down a German plane, a Junkers Ju-88 bomber, off the coast of Lowestoft in the UK. He shot down another Ju-88 bomber in Yarmouth, UK, in June. After this and other accomplishments, Junius's successes were being written about in various news outlets.

THE DIEPPE RAID

August 19, 1942, was considered one of the most heated air battles of the Second World War, and is known as the *Dieppe Raid*. Canadian soldiers had raided the German-occupied town of Dieppe in northern France that morning, located along the French coast. There were forty-eight squadrons flying Spitfires sent to fight there. The Royal Air Force and Royal Canadian Air Force flew close to three thousand aircraft for the mission, and ninety-seven of them were destroyed in the battle. As Allied pilots neared Dieppe, German air defences had about fifty German aircraft waiting for them, and the air battle quickly ensued as the force attacked at different points along the coast.

During combat, Junius attacked a Focke-Wulf Fw-190, also known as a *Würger*, knocking off a huge section of that aircraft's tail. But he quickly came under counterattack from another Fw-190, and that demolished almost the entire tail of his Spitfire. By then, Junius had lost sight of his wingman. He no longer had radio contact, so he returned to his squadron's base. The squadron's report from that day shows they couldn't believe that Junius was able to make it back with his aircraft so damaged. In total, Junius's squadron damaged or completely destroyed six enemy aircraft during the Dieppe Raid.

MORE MISSIONS

Just five days later, Junius was posted to 401 Squadron. By that time, he already had 112 flying hours behind him. He was being described as a reliable leader and people were noticing that he was great in combat.

B-17 Flying Fortress bomber.

Junius had to get used to the new squadron. He test-flew and took flights out to become accustomed to the new area in France. He flew with other pilots for formation practice. And he participated in his first "fighter sweep" on September 6. It was a mission where twelve aircraft from his squadron flew with thirty-six B-17 Flying Fortress bombers and protected them as they dropped bombs on a German aircraft factory at Méaulte, north of France.

On several missions, Junius flew as number three to Squadron Leader Keith Hodson. High-ranking officers normally took the number-one position in a squadron, while the number-three position was held by a squadron commander. On September 26, 1942, Junius's squadron, as well as two others, were completing a mission to protect thirty-six B-17 Flying Fortresses during an attack on the town of Morlaix, France. However, the weather at the time made that very hard. A very strong wind had blown the three squadrons way off course. Adding to that, heavy clouds blocked their view of the ground as they were returning. One of the squadrons, No. 133, lost all twelve of its aircraft. One had turned due to the weather and crashed, and the others were attacked by enemy fire.

It soon became clear that Junius's 401 Squadron would run out of fuel. When Junius was over the ocean, about sixty kilometres away from the English coast, he radioed to let his squadron know he was out of fuel. He told them he was going to jump out of his aircraft before it crashed. Junius was last seen doing a gradual dive in his parachute toward land. Because the other aircraft were also running out of fuel, they were unable to hover over Junius's aircraft to wait for air-sea rescue. The air-sea rescue was a search-and-rescue operation that would go out to find fallen members from aircraft and those lost at sea. Sending out this air-sea team was a normal practice.

After they refuelled, the squadron leader wanted to go back to try and search for Junius, but he was not allowed. The RCAF at first thought Junius was rescued by the Germans and taken as a **prisoner of war**. But on November 6, 1942, Junius's name appeared on the casualty list compiled by the RCAF. Beside his name is stated: *Killed* *on active service*. Junius was only twenty years old.

On October 6, 1943, a service and unveiling took place in London, England, with a memorial dedication at Biggin Hill, a famous fighter station, for pilots who had lost their lives during the Second World War. Junius was included in that dedication. His name is also inscribed on the Runnymede Memorial, located west of London, England. He had spent only a few years as a pilot in the RCAF. But in that short time, Pilot Officer Junius Hokan had made a remarkable impression on his squadron leaders and fellow pilots, and blazed a trail for the many pilots of colour who would come after him.

A newspaper clipping about Junius from the Toronto Star, April 1942.

Chapter 3: Flying Officer Junius Lyman Edward Hokan

4: INDIGENOUS FLYERS

Indigenous People make up about 5 percent of the population of Canada. That is over 1.8 million people. But they represent the largest community in need of air service, particularly in remote and isolated areas. It would have made good sense for some of the first pilots in Canada to be Indigenous, as Indigenous people know their lands well and have navigational skills that would help them as aviators. But throughout history, there have been many barriers in place against Indigenous people becoming pilots, like the cost of training and a lack of training nearby. Many of these barriers still exist.

INDIGENOUS PEOPLE IN CANADA

First Nations people, Inuit people, and the Métis are the three Indigenous groups in Canada. Indigenous people were the first inhabitants of the lands many of us know as Canada. They lived on the land for at least twelve thousand years, caring for and depending on the environment, before people from Europe first arrived in the 1500s.

After the arrival of **colonizers**, Indigenous people began to face many new struggles. They were forced off of their land, cut off from their way of life, and faced racism and abuse by the colonizers and the new government they established. Indigenous peoples are still fighting to reclaim their lands, cultures, and identities.

Many Indigenous communities are located in northern or remote areas. There are over 178 remote communities in Canada that are not connected to the North American electricity grid or natural gas resources. Some of these communities have no road access and some are only accessible by water or by plane, such as Aklavik, a small community in the Inuvik Region of the Northwest Territories, and Colville Lake in the Sahtu Region of the Northwest Territories, just north of the Arctic Circle.

Despite the many generations of historical challenges faced by Indigenous people, there are Indigenous flyers who managed to push through those obstacles and achieve careers in aviation. They have shown their dedication to supporting and empowering Indigenous people to chart their own legacies with a career in the sky. One such airman was Lieutenant James David Moses, who fought during the First World War.

JAMES DAVID MOSES

In February 1916, James David Moses enlisted to serve. At that time, he was a teacher from the Six Nations of the Grand River reserve in southern Ontario, and was actively engaged with the 114th Battalion. That was a local militia unit formed by up to three hundred Indigenous volunteers from the reserve and Haldimand County residents, as well as other troops.

Lt. James Moses, recruited from the Six Nations of the Grand River Reserve, c. 1916.

Chapter 4: Indigenous Flyers

James served as a Lieutenant with the 107th Battalion, the only fully integrated battalion in First World War that included Indigenous soldiers. Out of the more than nine hundred members, over half were of Indigenous ancestry, largely from Ontario and Manitoba. After he served for several months in France with the 107th battalion, James was moved to the 57th Squadron of the Royal Flying Corps to work as a gunner and an aerial observer. (A *gunner*'s job was to destroy enemy trenches by using explosives to collapse the structures. An *aerial observer*'s job was to find and gather information about the enemy's activities and supplies and bring it back to their squadron.)

Lt. James David Moses (back row, far right) with lieutenants of the 107th Infantry Battalion.

On April 1, 1918, James and his pilot, Douglas Trollip from South Africa, set out on a mission against the Germans, flying a DH-4 bomber. The two men never returned. A search effort was conducted, but the men's bodies were never found. James and Douglas were listed as *presumed dead*, among the more than 66,000 Canadians who died during the war. But James's bravery proved to others that a career in aviation for Indigenous people was very much possible.

The DH-4 was a two-seater bomber used during the First World War.

The Sky's the Limit!

FRED CARMICHAEL

Frederick James Carmichael (or Fred, as he is called) is a long-time aviator. He is a Gwich'in pilot from the North who has been flying the skies for seventy years. He is also known as the first Indigenous commercial pilot in the Canadian Arctic.

Fred grew up on a trapline, hunting animals and game, just outside of Aklavik in the Northwest Territories. He was about twelve years old when he began dreaming of flying, after he got a close look at a red Stinson aircraft on skis delivering supplies near his family's bush camp.

Fred recalled some of his experiences in a book by Danielle Metcalfe-Chenail, *Polar Winds: A Century of Flying the North*. When speaking of his experiences as an Indigenous pilot, Fred said, "It was quite a struggle… I come from a trapline. I drove a dog team and the next thing was an airplane…"

Gwich'in pilot Fred Carmichael was inducted into the Canadian Aviation Hall of Fame in 2016.

A mixed-ancestry person, he was often called names. "We didn't fit in as Indians or as whites," he explained, "so we learned to be independent." But he did not let the struggles or the name-calling stop him from pursuing a dream.

Fred Carmichael, the first Indigenous commercial pilot in the Arctic.

Chapter 4: Indigenous Flyers

Fred and the co-author of his children's book, Danielle Metcalfe-Chenail.

As a teenager, Fred left his childhood home of Aklavik, Northwest Territories, to save money for flying school. He went to Edmonton, Alberta, but always knew he would return to help his community. Fred would fly hunters, their supplies, and sometimes entire dogsled teams to their camps. He worked with reindeer herders, flew medical personnel and pregnant women to hospitals when required, and helped with search-and-rescue missions to help find missing tourists and locals.

Fred started his own aviation company, and he made it a point to hire and train local Indigenous pilots. This was another way he gave back to his community. Fred acknowledges that he had many great mentors and teachers along the way, and he pays it forward by supporting the next generation of aviators. Many of those trained by Fred have gone on to enjoy successful careers with aviation firms across the country.

Fred faced many obstacles on his journey, like trying to apply for licenses and being outright rejected. But he kept at it until he was successful. Today, Fred is one of the most celebrated pilots in the Indigenous community and in Canada. He is a member of the Order of Canada, and was inducted into the Order of the Northwest Territories. Fred was also awarded an honorary doctorate from the University of Saskatchewan. In 2016, Fred was inducted into Canada's Aviation Hall of Fame. He even co-wrote an award-winning children's book about his amazing life and career, *Freddie the Flyer*, with Metcalfe-Chenail, in 2023.

Fred is considered a pioneer of aviation and business, and is seen as a leader in his community. If you fly into Aklavik, you will likely land at the Aklavik/Fred Carmichael Airport! While Fred takes great care when flying and has accomplished a lot throughout his seven decades of working in the air, he is modest about his many accomplishments.

KIMBERLY BALLANTYNE

Kimberly Ballantyne wanted to be a pilot from the age of four. She started on a path toward that dream when she was sixteen. Then, at thirty-six, she saw that dream come true. In the process, she made history by becoming the first Indigenous woman pilot in Opaskwayak Cree Nation. But like many pilots from underrepresented communities, her path was not always easy.

Cree Pilot Kimberly Ballantyne.

Kimberly is a treaty member of Opaskwayak Cree Nation, Manitoba. She grew up in an isolated part of the community called Umpherville. A Cree speaker, Kimberly was raised by her maternal grandparents, Flora and Malcolm Crane. They were her biggest supporters. They inspired Kimberly to complete her education.

Kimberly recalls her home being filled with laughter. Her grandparents and Uncle Danny would often joke around with each other. But Kimberly says that like many Indigenous families in her community at that time, their housing was crowded, contained mould, and had no running water. There were many societal obstacles, like racism, poverty, and abuse. Despite the many odds stacked against her, Kimberly had a dream.

Kim's grandparents Flora and Malcolm Crane inspired her to dream.

Kimberly was exposed to aviation at an early age, because she lived between two airports: Missinippi Airways and The Pas Airport. She remembered always looking to the sky and seeing aircraft flying overhead. When she told her grandfather Malcolm she wanted to be a pilot, he encouraged Kimberly to follow her dreams.

Kimberly's grandparents were very traditional. She refers to her life as *walking in between two worlds*, as she lived between their very traditional ways and modern societal ways. Her grandparents worked very hard and lived off the land. Kimberly grew up fishing, hunting, and watching her grandparents harvest deer or moose hide. She ate traditional foods, such as moose meat and fried pickerel. Her grandmother also handmade all of her outfits. Yet her grandparents also knew the world was changing. They encouraged Kimberly to succeed in education so that she could go out and achieve whatever she wanted.

In 2004, Kimberly graduated from Margaret Barbour Collegiate Institute with her diploma. She was the first person in her family to graduate high school. When she was twenty-three, Kimberly had to leave her community in order to further her education. It was very scary, to move to the city. All Kimberly had when she left for Winnipeg to attend the University of Manitoba was a bag of clothes, a television, and a blow-up mattress. But she was on a path to becoming a pilot.

Kim Ballantyne flew a two-seater plane built by Jill Oakes, a member of Ninety-Nines Manitoba.

Kimberly completed her Bachelor of Arts Degree in February 2014, another monumental achievement—she is also the first in her family to complete university. She had many responsibilities as she pursued her flight training. Money was a big issue. Kimberly had to withdraw from **ground school** several times because of the cost. Still, she continued to work hard and refused to give up.

Eventually, in 2022, Kimberly earned her private pilot license. In 2023, she passed her commercial pilot license exam, and began working on the flight test for her full commercial pilot license. In August 2024, Kimberly

Chapter 4: Indigenous Flyers

completed her fifty-fourth flight towards obtaining that commercial pilot's license, and continues to keep working towards that goal. She wants to provide a good life for her two kids. By her own example, she is showing them what hard work can do, and that dedication and discipline will help to achieve your dreams.

ROBYN SHLACHETKA & RAVEN BEARDY

Robyn Shlachetka and Raven Beardy are two Indigenous pilots who were raised in northern Manitoba. They are also longtime friends. Robyn is from Wabowden and Raven is from Shamattawa First Nation. They are in the flying profession *and* in the helping profession. This pair landed in Canada's history books when they became the first female Indigenous medevac team.

Medevac is short for *medical evacuation,* which is a term used to refer to taking people from one place to another for medical care. The medevac team airlifts—or evacuates—patients to a hospital or other medical facility. This is also called a *med flight*.

Before the flight takes off, the medevac team makes sure the patient is prepared for travel, checking that the patient is secured and not too sick to fly.

First Officer Raven Beardy (left) and Captain Robyn Shlachetka (right).

Robyn and her father flying in his Cessna 170B.

That may mean giving them medicine or taking care of other needs to keep them safe while flying. During the flight, the medical team continues to observe the patient.

Flying into remote northern communities for medevac services isn't an easy job. There are many challenges, such as periods of extreme cold, darkness, and harsh weather like blackout conditions due to lack of lighting on the runway, and whiteout conditions due to blizzards. As a part of a previous medevac team in Manitoba, Captain Robyn and First Officer Raven became role models to young Indigenous girls everywhere.

Robyn Shlachetka is a Medevac Captain. She was born in Thompson, Manitoba, raised in Wabowden, and is registered with Pimicikamak, a Cree First Nation in Cross Lake, Manitoba. In 1989, her family was evacuated from their home due to a large fire. Her father was a **bush pilot** at that time. They didn't have a lot of resources, but her father's boss flew them to a place of refuge at Utik Lake.

Robyn, who was seven at the time, remembers being in the aircraft with her father and sister that day. It was then that she knew she wanted to fly. Not only that, but she wanted to help people, too.

Robyn shared this dream with a teacher. The teacher told her that girls do not become pilots and that she should drop the idea. But Robyn was fearless, and her father encouraged Robyn and her sister to follow their passions. By age eighteen, Robyn had enrolled in flight school and finished her private pilot licence alongside an all-female cadet training program. She successfully finished her training one year later.

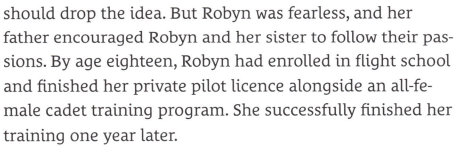

Robyn flying the Navajo PA31.

During flight training, Robyn experienced many challenges. However, she demonstrated great skill, proving she was a talented flyer. In the early days of her flying career, it was scary at times. She was flying in the North, often over rough terrain and in harsh weather. Now that she is an experienced pilot with incredible skill, the weather and the terrain don't bother her anymore. She loves her work.

Robyn was a medevac pilot for over six years. She loved the thrill of it. A day at her job sometimes consisted of shifts as long as eleven or fourteen hours for two weeks at a time. She was normally accompanied by her first officer and one or two paramedics or nurses. Sometimes their job required them to fly throughout the night. She was once part of a flight to Nunavut when there was only thirty minutes of daylight. But the crew successfully navigated those conditions.

Robyn's good friend Raven Beardy is also a fearless flyer. She started her flying career as a First Officer on a Navajo with Missinippi Airways for six months before moving on to the King Air, flying medevac. Raven became interested in flying when she was medevaced from her community as a young girl. She wondered if someone who looked like her could fly a plane like the one that took her to safety that day.

Raven was adopted by an RCMP officer and his wife and grew up in Shamattawa. Living up in the Arctic enabled Raven to participate in traditional activities. It also made her appreciate both First Nations and Inuit culture, and how they are different and the same in many ways.

Growing up in isolated communities, Raven recognized the vital role of the aviation industry. It was how her community received groceries and medical supplies for the nursing stations, and how the teachers

First Officer Raven Beardy with an aircraft from Air Care, a company that transports medicine.

Chapter 4: Indigenous Flyers

53

and construction workers got in and out for work.

Raven remembers an incident that took place when she was young. There was a bad snowstorm in Shamattawa and the power went out. Someone in her community needed to be medevaced out but there was no way to light up the runway. Everybody got their snowmobiles out and lined up along the runway, shining their headlights so that the pilots could see and safely land. That event affected Raven and made her want to be involved in things like that.

Raven went through a three-year Aviation College Diploma Program with First Nations Technical Institute in Ontario. She graduated with a commercial license, multi-engine and IFR rating. During her studies, she experienced moments of isolation and loneliness being away from home. When Raven was a participant in search-and-rescue training in a Hercules and a twin otter in Rankin Inlet, Nunavut, she made a visit to her parents in the summer. The two pilots flying that aircraft were both female. That encouraged Raven, and she realized that she could do that too.

Raven and her sister.

The Sky's the Limit!

Raven is no longer flying as a medevac pilot. She is now a first officer based out of Iqaluit, Nunavut, and flies an ATR 42 with Canadian North, an airline that services the Arctic. When she is not working in the sky, Raven likes to fly with her father. He owns a Cessna 180 on floats and a Piper Warrior PA-28. He has his private pilot license and he now flies for fun whenever he can.

An ATR 42 similar to the one Raven flies with Canadian North.

Both Robyn and Raven now live and fly in different areas of Manitoba. Robyn is in Thompson and Raven is in Winnipeg. They cherish the time they spent working together, helping people in crisis, saving lives, and navigating the skies as friends.

Robyn and Raven took on the challenges of flying in the North, and today, they continue doing what they dreamed of as children. For them, their work in the sky is like giving back to their communities, and they encourage other Indigenous youth to aim for a career in the sky.

Chapter 4: Indigenous Flyers

5: WOMEN IN AVIATION

Historically, women had to fight for their place in aviation. For hundreds of years they were largely absent, particularly when it came to the military. However, Canadian women have contributed and served in war efforts. During the North-West Resistance of 1885, which started after the Métis people won a battle for their land in present-day Saskatchewan and Alberta, the government feared an uprising by the Métis people and their Indigenous allies who were defending their culture and their lands. By order of the government, twelve women were employed as nurses. Loretta Miller was the first to arrive at the Field Hospital in Saskatoon on May 12, 1885. These women were considered officially part of the military for the first time in Canada.

Eileen Vollick in her flight gear.

Later on, during the First and Second World Wars, women held a few military roles, mainly clerical and medical. Now, women serve in all three branches of the military: the Royal Canadian Navy, the Canadian Army, and the Royal Canadian Air Force. But it wasn't until 1989 that women were permitted to hold major military positions and participate in combat. And it wasn't until 2001 that women were able to work in submarines.

Prior to this, women's skills and knowledge were not seen as good enough. That was also true when it came to aviation training. But on March 13, 1928, when Eileen Vollick of Wiarton, Ontario, was just nineteen years old, she became the first licensed female pilot in Canada. Because no other woman had ever applied to become a pilot before, Eileen had to write a letter to the government just to get permission to fly commercially. She eventually received a yes. When she passed the Government Civil Aviation Examination, Eileen became the seventy-seventh licensed pilot in Canada. And her accomplishments paved a path for other women to dream. The first Canadian female pilot to be hired by a commercial airline was Rosella Bjornson in 1973. Today,

Eileen Vollick was the only female student at Elliott Air Service.

Eileen Vollick was a member of the **Ninety-Nines**, a worldwide group made up of female pilots. Amelia Earhart was the first woman to fly solo across the Atlantic Ocean and was one of the people who started the very first chapter of the Ninety-Nines in Long Island, New York, in 1929. The organization continued to grow and now has chapters in over thirty-five countries around the world.

The first Canadian chapter was formed back in 1951 with just nine members. It continues to grow each year and has surpassed two thousand members. Ninety Nines are not only pilots, but also students in training and women who work in other areas of aviation.

Chapter 5: Women in Aviation

> "As I sat in the cockpit I felt quite at home, fear never entered my head and when I saw the earth recede as the winged monster roared and soared skyward, and the familiar scenes below became a vast panorama of checker-boarded fields, neatly arranged toy houses, and silvery threads of streams, the pure joy of it, gave me a thrill which is known only to the air-man who wings his way among the fleecy clouds."
>
> – Eilleen Vollick, describing her first flight, *Owen Sound Sun Times*, 2008

women make up about 10 percent of Canada's pilots. That includes pilots from across all categories: student pilots; recreational, private, and commercial pilots; and airline transport pilots. In 2023, 12 percent of pilot licences issued were to women.

Over the decades, women and girls have been finding work in aviation. They are not only pilots flying the skies, but they are also making their mark in other areas of aviation, such as engineering, science, and technology.

Rosella Bjornson's first flight as a First Officer on F28 with Transair, Winnipeg, Manitoba, June 1973.

ELIZABETH MACGILL

Elizabeth Muriel Gregory MacGill, known as *Elsie*, was born in Vancouver, British Columbia, in March 1905. The first woman engineer in Canada, she earned a degree in electrical engineering and became the first woman to earn a master's degree in aeronautical engineering in 1929.

That same year, Elsie was diagnosed with polio. The doctors told her she might never walk again. But from her wheelchair, Elsie did not give up. She used two metal canes and taught herself how to walk again. After receiving her postgraduate degree at a Boston college, Elsie returned to Canada and started a job as an assistant aeronautical engineer at Fairchild Aircraft Limited. There, she worked on aircraft designs. She became the first Canadian woman to design a plane.

A portrait of Elsie MacGill, 1938.

In 1938, Elsie secured a role as a chief engineer at the Canadian Car & Foundry in Fort William, Ontario, during the Second World War, and was in charge of the production of fighter planes for the RCAF. The single-seat, single-engine, **monoplane** fighter aircraft, originally designed by Sir Sydney Camm in the 1930s, was known as the Hawker Hurricane. And engineer Elsie soon became known as the *Queen of the Hurricanes*.

The first mass of Hawker Hurricanes, designed with modifications for flying in cold weather, took off in January 1940. These planes were vital during the Second World War when Britain was protecting itself from the German air force, what was known as the *Battle of Britain*. Within three

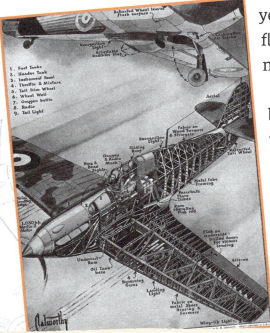
A blueprint of the Hawker Hurricane M1.

years of that first Hurricane taking flight, Elsie's team had produced 1,400 more Hawker Hurricanes.

For all her accomplishments, Elsie became the first woman accepted into the Engineering Institute of Canada. She received the Order of Canada, which is the country's second highest honour. She was also inducted into the Canadian Aviation Hall of Fame and the Canadian Science and Engineering Hall of Fame.

JENNIFER GAWOR

Jennifer Gawor is a private pilot. She obtained two private pilot licenses starting at the age of sixteen through scholarships with the Air Cadet League of Canada (see sidebar on page 24). She earned her glider pilot licence in 2003, training on the Schweizer SGS 2-33, and her private pilot licence in 2004, training on the Diamond DA20 Katana.

Jennifer had been fascinated by outer space since she was a little girl. She would go to the library every chance she got to learn about the solar system, astronomy, and space travel. That ignited her imagination and excitement for science and discovery. When she was thirteen, she began researching what training she would need to become an astronaut. She discovered that almost all astronauts start out as pilots.

When Jennifer joined air cadets, there were not many girls from her high school thinking about aviation. She grew up in a lower-middle-class family in Scarborough, Ontario. She had many challenges growing up, as someone living with Attention Deficit Hyperactivity Disorder (ADHD), a neurodiverse condition that can affect how a person processes information. Jennifer's school life was unsupportive and she was bullied a lot as a kid. But she refused to let that stop her from pursuing her dreams.

Jennifer Gawor's photo gallery.

Jennifer loved the structure of air cadets. She got to meet fighter pilots, travel to the US, and fly in gliders on weekends. These experiences boosted Jennifer's confidence and self-esteem.

Jennifer currently works for a college and an aerospace hub in Toronto, Ontario, as a digital media coordinator. She describes her path to becoming a pilot as one of determination, resilience, and overcoming adversity.

One of Jennifer's biggest moments was when she was on her last solo flight the evening before graduation. She was

The **Schweizer SGS 2-33** is a popular glider for training. It is considered to be rugged and easy to navigate. It is a two-seat, high-wing glider and is known for its durability and forgiving flight characteristics, making it ideal for new pilots.

flying in the airport practice area and there was a beautiful sunset igniting the entire sky. It was a dreamlike moment for her. She said to herself, *You did it, Jen. You finally got here*. She felt a huge sense of freedom and accomplishment.

The **Diamond DA20 Katana** is designed to be reliable and safe. It is a two-seat, single-engine light aircraft designed for general aviation use. It's known for its sleek design, fuel efficiency, and ease of handling. It is commonly used for flight training as well as personal and recreational flying. Its modern design makes it popular among flight schools and private pilots.

SERGEANT ALISHA FISHER

Sergeant Alisha Fisher is an aviation maintenance technician. On a typical day, this might mean performing a variety of tasks, such as solving any electrical or mechanical problems with an aircraft. She might also repair parts of the aircraft, like wings and brakes, and replace broken parts. This kind of work used to be thought of as a "man's job." However, Alisha loves her work and she tries to be a role model for her daughter, Blake.

Alisha joined the RCAF in 2007 as an Aviation Systems (AVN) Technician from Halifax, Nova Scotia. In 2009, she was posted to Cold Lake, Alberta, the home of fighter pilot training. There she worked in the 410 Tactical Fighter Operational Training Squadron. After working in many different positions, she was promoted to master corporal in 2015. That means she is in a position of leadership, overseeing other corporals. Alisha spent four years working as a technical instructor before she was again promoted and became Sergeant Fisher—a senior rank.

Her Excellency the Right Honourable Julie Payette, 29th Governor General of Canada, herself a former astronaut, presents the Medal of Bravery to then Corporal Fisher (left), at Rideau Hall, 2018.

In March of 2015, when she was still a corporal, Alisha saved one of her colleagues from drowning. They were at the ocean near San Diego, California, when her colleague got caught in a riptide at Torrey Pines State Beach Park and was struggling to make it to the shore. Alisha noticed and immediately sprang into action. She swam out to him quickly and held him afloat. Finally, a lifeguard reached them and helped bring her colleague to safety.

In 2016, Alisha was awarded the Medal of Bravery by the Governor General of Canada for this act.

ALLISON RUMBOLT

Captain Allison Rumbolt sits next to her longtime friend, First Officer Zoe Webb.

Allison Rumbolt is originally from Mary's Harbour, a small town of a few hundred residents in Newfoundland and Labrador.

Allison's father worked in operations at an airline where her mother was a part-time employee. So Allison was at the airport frequently and became interested in aviation early on. Pilots would sometimes let her board the planes and observe their "workplace."

Allison met First Officer Zoe Webb when she was about eleven years old, and that relationship opened up a window to the world of flying helicopters. She and Zoe went on to be close friends. As an adult, Allison worked her way through the ranks, eventually becoming a captain. To become a captain, a pilot starts out as a first officer, and after they spend some time in the job, must take a course, and pass a few tests.

After starting her career in Labrador flying through the bush, Allison went through the steps and became Captain Rumbolt. She was the very first female captain to fly a Sikorsky S-92 helicopter for Cougar Helicopters, a company that operates a fleet of helicopters for search-and-rescue and offshore transportation out of St. John's, Newfoundland and Labrador.

The date June 9, 2021, was a memorable one for Allison. It was the day she came full circle and got to sit in the cockpit with her friend and mentor Zoe as part of an all-female crew.

Allison's workday usually starts about an hour before she is ready to take off in the aircraft. During that hour, she must complete flight inspections to make sure the aircraft is working efficiently. She must also check the weather conditions for that day. She and her crew will then get the details about their **flight plan**. That might include information about the ship or oil rig that they will be landing

The **Sikorsky S-92** is a medium-sized, twin-engine helicopter. It is American made and was built for civil and military helicopter markets. It is often used to perform missions such as search-and-rescue and offshore oil transportation. The powerful S-92 evolved from the Sikorsky S-70 US Army Black Hawk and the SH-60 US Navy Seahawk helicopters.

Chapter 5: Women in Aviation

on, how much fuel they will need, and how many passengers they will be transporting.

Plans may change if there is a shift in weather or other issues arise. At the end of each day there is paperwork to be done, and the aircraft needs to go through an engine rinse, to remove dirt and saltwater buildup and ensure the engine continues to work well.

Allison in the cockpit, flying through the clouds.

6: A NEW GENERATION OF AVIATORS

In the past, the doors to a future in aviation were not open to everyone. But thanks to the trailblazers you've read about in this book, many obstacles have been removed, or are moving out of the way.

Women, people of colour, newcomers to Canada, and so many other previously underrepresented groups are following the paths that lead to a career in aviation. Private and commercial piloting are good options, even for people living with various disabilities. In the RCAF, there are over a hundred different roles now available. Aviators are also involved in all kinds of jobs with humanitarian missions, private enterprise, government, education, engineering, and more. The more the field opens up, the more the diversity of Canadians in aviation will shine.

Let's meet a few amazing people who are new to the field of Canadian aviation!

MOHAMED SAMANTER

Captain Mohamed Samanter started exploring an aviation career in high school. He was the youngest of four brothers growing up in Ottawa. His family came from humble beginnings as newcomers to Canada. Mohamed played a lot of sports, including high school football, and was fortunate to have a guidance counsellor who took the time to help him explore the path to becoming a pilot. Mohamed booked an introductory flight lesson at the Ottawa Flying Club to try it out. After that first flight, he knew he wanted that flight deck to be his future office.

Mohamed sitting on the steps of his small plane.

Mohamed became a charter pilot, and one important event in his career taught him a lot about the strength of community. His Canadian aviation company assigned him to fly to a remote area of South Sudan in Africa. His task was to pick up a team working for an organization that helps people in need.

Mohamed was to land the plane on an airstrip called Old Fangak, a remote marshland in South Sudan. During the wet season, sometimes the airstrip can became unusable.

When Mohamed and his co-pilot approached the airstrip, they hit a wet patch hidden by tall trees at the end of the runway. As the plane slid, their gear got stuck in the mud and started sinking. Mohamed and his co-pilot shut down the engines and left the plane. They tied rope to the bottom of the plane and tried to pull it out of the mud, but it was too heavy. Villagers noticed the stuck plane and tried to help, but still it was no use.

Mohamed's new friends offer him help on the Old Fangak airstrip in South Sudan.

The Sky's the Limit!

When the sun started to set, the villagers offered the pilots a place to stay for the night in their community.

By the next morning, word had to travelled. When Mohamed and his co-pilot got back to the plane, about a hundred locals were waiting to help move the 13-tonne plane. With rope and many hands, they were able to pull the plane out of the mud!

Afterwards, there was a celebration, and Mohamed and his co-pilot gave the villagers gifts to show their appreciation. Mohamed said the beauty of the African spirit was definitely on display that day. Mohamed is now a captain flying commercial planes in Ontario.

ARDEL SMITH

Ardel Smith is the first Black helicopter pilot from the historic Black communities of Nova Scotia. He grew up in Cole Harbour and has roots in North Preston, the largest historic Black settlement in Canada.

Ardel's interest in airplanes began as a young boy of about five years old, when his father, Danny, started taking him to watch the air shows in Shearwater, an RCAF base located in Dartmouth, Nova Scotia. Later, during a family vacation in the United States, Ardel went on a helicopter ride, then on another during a field trip as part of a local summer camp. Neither ride was very long, but Ardel said that was all it took to hook him on helicopters. He knew then that he wanted to fly them.

Chapter 6: A New Generation of Aviators

Ardel Smith inside his helicopter.

Ardel searched through a magazine directory of helicopter companies to find out about flight schools. In 1999, he went to British Columbia, where he attended his first flight school. Later, he enrolled at Canadian Helicopters flight school in Buttonville, Ontario. After graduating, he got a non-piloting job with a company called Four Seasons Aviation.

Ardel spent several years working in aviation between Ontario and Nova Scotia before he eventually secured a position as a pilot with Four Seasons. The company had a contract with Global News. Part of Ardel's role included flying the reporters and camera operators around the Greater Toronto Area so that they could gather footage.

After his work with the company, Ardel went to Yellowknife in the Northwest Territories and flew with a small helicopter company there for five years. Ardel said that working in Yellowknife helped him sharpen his skills as a helicopter pilot. Then in 2011, Ardel returned home to Nova Scotia to work as a helicopter pilot for the Nova Scotia Department of Natural Resources and Renewables, where he continues to serve.

In his role with the department, Ardel does everything

from forest and wildlife surveys to searching for missing people. He collaborates with law enforcement and emergency services whenever necessary. For example, he is often one of the first on scene during a forest fire, and works to help stop the fire from getting out of control.

Through his work, it has been important for Ardel to connect with and give back to his community. He enjoys taking part in community events, youth outreach, and career days at local schools. He finds talking to young people about his journey quite rewarding, and says he wants to motivate youth to follow their dreams. The students are always proud and excited to see someone from their community reach such heights. And in turn, Ardel is always inspired by their great enthusiasm and energy.

During the annual North Preston Days event in 2022, Ardel landed his helicopter in the Arnold D. Johnston Sports Field and let the students climb on and explore his helicopter. The following year, Ardel flew his helicopter above the event in a show of community togetherness and pride. Allowing youth to see someone from their community who looks like them achieving their goals is a powerful way to inspire the next generation of aviators.

Ardel does everything from wildlife surveys to helping fight forest fires, from his helicopter.

Chapter 6: A New Generation of Aviators

DANIEL REID

Airbus A330 Pilot Daniel Reid.

Daniel, whose official title is now First A330 Reid, has been working in the sky for ten years. He began his career in aviation by becoming first officer, and later became a captain. Daniel can't remember a time when he didn't dream of becoming a pilot. He had other passions, like veterinary sciences. But the skies called to him.

Daniel was born in Kingston, Jamaica, and spent most of his childhood there before moving to Brampton, Ontario. As an only child, he was very close with his large extended family, who now live all over the world. Much of his childhood was spent playing sports and video games, and enjoying time with his family. Not having any siblings could have made his childhood lonely, but Daniel is grateful for all of that quality time with his parents.

After graduating from high school, Daniel completed a Bachelor in Aviation Technology at Seneca College. Following that, he got a job fuelling aircraft and worked in airline crew scheduling. While he worked, he trained for his flight instructor certification at Brampton Flight Centre.

Daniel's first job once he received this certification was conducting aerial photo surveys. That role includes tasks such as collecting images, data, and geological information from an aircraft or a helicopter. It might also include analyzing that information for research and other purposes. The job gave Daniel enough flying experience to land a position at Porter Airlines as a first officer on the Dash 8-Q400. After four years, he transitioned to captain, and then to relief pilot on the Airbus A330 with a different airline.

The first all-Black flight crew in Porter Airlines history. Left to right: Tiffany Ruiz-Stonge, Mohamed Samanter, Eden Otti, Daniel Reid.

Daniel's parents were a big influence on his career. Daniel's father, who flew helicopters in the military before working as an airline pilot, introduced Daniel to aviation and helped him along the journey, sharing his technical knowledge and giving Daniel emotional support.

When Daniel attended college, he didn't see many other people who looked like him in his training; at graduation, their class of fifty included only five people of colour.

The path wasn't all smooth for Daniel. The work was hard. There were times when he considered giving up. But his parents continued to support and guide him, even when his mother thought a job on the ground instead of thirty thousand feet in the air might have been better!

Daniel was working with Captain Mohamed Samanter in 2023 when the two of them made news along with two Black flight attendants, becoming the first all-Black crew in Porter Airlines' sixteen-year history!

Chapter 6: A New Generation of Aviators

APPENDIX A: CANADA'S AVIATION MUSEUMS

Aviation museums are of huge importance in Canada because they preserve and protect the history of flight in our country and around the world. Below are just some of the country's aviation museums that you can explore. Which ones would you like to go to?

ATLANTIC CANADA AVIATION MUSEUM

Despite the momentous event of the Flight of the *Silver Dart*, before this museum was built, the history of Atlantic Canada's early aviation had slowly started to fade away. Important **artifacts** from the past were becoming lost. That made it necessary and urgent to gather and preserve what was left, to ensure the next generation of aviation enthusiasts would learn about it. That goal led to the development of this museum.

Today, the Atlantic Canada Aviation Museum, located on Sky Boulevard in Enfield, near the Halifax Stanfield International Airport, is one of the only museums in the region dedicated to preserving the history and legacy of aviation. It was formed in 1977 by a group of eager volunteers and opened to the public in 1985.

As you walk through the museum, you will see hundreds of artifacts such as uniforms, badges, books, and aircraft that span from the very early days of flight through to modern aircraft and other technology.

The museum is home to many great pieces of history, such as the Canadair CF-5 Freedom Fighter, built between 1968 and 1975. The Canadian Air Force took on 135 CF-5s and they flew in Canadian service with squadrons 419, 433, and 434 to help support the country's commitment to NATO (a political alliance of the Euro-Atlantic area). In 1995, Canada retired its Freedom Fighters. Most were stored away, but some were sold to other countries and given to aviation museums.

The Atlantic Canada Aviation Museum experienced much growth over the years. In 1995 a new hangar was attached to its original building, giving the museum an extra 14,000 square feet of space to display its wide variety of exhibits, aircraft, and other pieces of history.

CANADA AVIATION AND SPACE MUSEUM

The Canada Aviation and Space Museum is located in Ottawa, Ontario, just five minutes away from where the prime minister lives at Sussex Drive. Situated on a former military air base, it focuses on international aviation dating back to 1909.

The museum has a display of over a dozen different gas and jet turbine engines so that visitors can learn about their history and technology. Visitors can also learn what life is like at the International Space Station.

CANADIAN MUSEUM OF FLIGHT

The Canadian Museum of Flight has its beginnings in the 1970s, when a group of aviation enthusiasts got together to keep some historic aircraft in Canada rather than seeing them all being sent to the US and Europe. The museum moved to its current location at the Langley Regional Airport in British Columbia in the 1990s. Over twenty-five civilian and military jets, gliders, aircraft, and helicopters are on display here. Of those, six have been restored to flight condition. The museum has the only displayed Handley Page Hampden, a Second World War Royal Air Force bomber, in the world. This museum encourages visitors to touch many of their exhibits—a truly "hands on" experience!

MONTREAL AVIATION MUSEUM

The Montreal Aviation Museum is housed in the historic Old Stone Barn on the Macdonald Campus of McGill University in Sainte-Anne-de-Bellevue, Quebec. Opened in 1998, this museum spotlights the military aviation heritage of Quebec and other parts of Canada. If you visit, you can view a replica of the Blériot XI Scarabée, the first plane to be flown over a city in Canada—by Count Jacques de Lesseps in 1910, over Montreal.

NATIONAL AIR FORCE MUSEUM OF CANADA

Located on the north side of 8 Wing Trenton in Quinte West, Ontario, the National Air Force Museum of Canada, established in 1894, is "dedicated to preserving and telling the history of Canadian military aviation." A sprawling location, at over 75,000 square feet of space in a 16-acre aviation park, this destination will allow you to visit a Burgess Dunne, a Hercules CC130, and a fully restored Second World War Halifax Bomber.

NO. 6 RCAF DUNNVILLE MUSEUM

The No. 6 RCAF Dunnville Museum sits on the site of the No. 6 Service Flying Training School in Dunnville, Ontario. The location was built to train pilots to fly fighter aircraft as part of the British Commonwealth Air Training Plan (BCATP) during the Second World War. Among other things, the site includes five hangars and three double runways. The musem's collection includes vintage aircraft, realistic models, and flight simulators. It is one of very few museums that collects and preserves artifacts and training aircraft from the British Commonwealth Air Training Plan—an important part of Canadian aviation history.

ROYAL AVIATION MUSEUM OF WESTERN CANADA

The Royal Aviation Museum of Western Canada is located in Winnipeg, Manitoba. It holds one of the biggest bush plane collections in the world. It also holds an extensive collection of aircraft, including military and passenger planes, and thousands of aviation artifacts, as well as over sixty thousand images. It was begun in 1974 when a group of aviation enthusiasts rescued a Bellanca Aircruiser from the bush in Northern Ontario. Its new facility is 86,000 square feet of artifacts, aircraft, and information!

SASKATCHEWAN AVIATION MUSEUM

A relatively new museum, the Saskatchewan Aviation Museum was founded in 2007 at the Saskatoon International Airport in Saskatchewan. It houses artifacts to remember and commemorate the province's aviation pioneers. Displays feature bush planes and Second World War memorabilia, including a bright yellow de Havilland DH82C Tiger Moth, which you can book a flight on, as well flight simulators.

APPENDIX B: FLIGHT SIMULATORS

If you really want to see what it's like to fly a plane, but you're not old enough to start training, you're in luck! If you're aged twelve or older, you can try a flight simulator. Some places that specialize in aviation and aviation training have these amazing machines. They are fake cockpits that you sit in, just like a pilot would. Using the controls, you can pretend to fly, watch the scenery change through the front "windshield" (a screen), and feel all the motions and vibrations of a real plane—all without leaving the ground! You even get to see the navigation panel and learn how to take off and land.

Learning to fly can be exciting and scary at the same time. Handling a plane or helicopter that can climb thousands of miles into the air takes a lot of training and skill. Pilots need to be able to navigate in all kinds of conditions, such as darkness, rain, and fog. With a flight simulator, aviation students can learn to fly in all types of scenarios without any real passengers onboard.

One example is the Redbird Flight Simulator (FMX 1000). It is a full-motion, three-axis flight training device.

Professional pilots from around the world can go to places like Montreal to train on a simulator because they are programmed to look like the cockpit of a specific aircraft, like the Airbus 220 or the Boeing 737. The Federal Aviation Administration now accepts one hour in an approved simulator to be equal to one hour of training in the air.

Other crew besides the pilots can also benefit from flight simulator training, such as riflemen training on military aircraft. These machines can also be used to run drills, such as planning for an emergency evacuation in the event of a plane crash.

APPENDIX C: HOW TO BECOME A PILOT IN CANADA

While a person is in training to become a pilot, they can carry what's called a *student pilot license* from as young as age fourteen. But with a student pilot license, they must also have a flight instructor with them whenever they fly. Once they are fully trained and ready, they can begin to conduct some flights on their own. Some pilots may carry a *recreational pilot certificate*. This allows them to fly certain kinds of aircraft with small numbers of people on board, like a single family or a small sports team.

There are many different paths to obtaining a pilot's license, and the steps you take will vary, depending on what kind of pilot you want to be. For example, if you are interested in flying for fun or with a friend, you can train for a *recreational license* by attending a local flight centre or a flight academy in your area. You have to complete at least twenty-five hours of flying. That includes fifteen hours with a trainer and ten hours by yourself. In order to get the *recreational pilot permit*, you have to pass a written exam and a flight test. You don't have to go to ground school for the recreational license, but the extra training could help.

If you want to fly professionally, obtaining a *private pilot license* would be the next step. With a recreational license, you are only permitted to have one other person with you. And you can only fly in a small, single-engine aircraft. But with a private pilot license, you can have a full flight of passengers onboard. You have to complete at least forty-five hours of flying, which includes twenty-five hours with a trainer and fifteen hours on your own. You also have to pass a written exam and a flight test, as well as complete forty hours of ground school.

To qualify for a *commercial pilot's license*, you must first have your private pilot license. Then you have to complete eighty hours of ground school, sixty-five hours of flight training (thirty-five hours with a trainer and thirty hours on your own). In addition, you need to be "time building." That means you need to make sure you fly a minimum required number of hours for your license. You also have to score a minimum of 60 percent on your written exam before receiving the license. Altogether, you need two hundred hours in flight, one hundred hours as **pilot in command**, and twenty hours of cross-country flights under your belt to qualify for a commercial pilot's license.

In addition to the examinations and the time spent flying the aircraft, you also need to go through a series of standard tests to check your vision, hearing, mental strength, and physical fitness. You also have to clear three medical categories to ensure you are healthy and fit for soaring to those high heights.

Many young people dream of flying high, but not everyone gets to do it. If you have a passion and a dream, keep working hard to achieve your goals—the sky's the limit!

GLOSSARY

ace A combat pilot with at least five downed enemy aircraft.

aerodynamics The study of the motion of air, and how objects move through the air, particularly when they come in contact with a solid object, such as an airplane's wing.

aerospace The industry of building aircraft, vehicles, and equipment to fly the skies or to be sent into space.

aircraft Vehicles or machines such as an airplane, glider, or helicopter that can travel through the air and transport passengers and goods.

air force The part of a country's military and armed forces that fight using aircraft and protect the country's airspace.

anti-flak Also called *anti-aircraft fire*. A term used to describe combat pilots' defenses against enemy fire, such as aircraft guns. The term was first used during the Second World War.

artifact An object of historical and cultural significance.

aviation The designing, building, and flying of various aircraft.

battalion A troop of soldiers that form part of a large brigade.

bush pilot An aviator who works and flies in Canada's remote northern regions, flying small propeller aircraft. They provide transportation for passengers and cargo.

colonizers People, groups, or governments that occupy and settle in a place that doesn't belong to them.

conscription Mandatory enlistment into the military, with no choice.

draft — A notice from the government to join the military without an option to refuse.

flight plan — A plan made by a pilot prior to flying an aircraft, and filed with the aviation authority, considering many factors to ensure a safe flight. These include the weather en route and at the destination, fuel requirements, the number of passengers and crew onboard, an alternate airport if required, altitude and route of the flight, departure and landing times and other important information.

ground school — One of the first steps of flight training, where students learn about things like how weather affects flying, aircraft instruments, and aerodynamics (how aircraft are able to stay in the air). Transport Canada requires at least forty hours of ground school for a Private Pilot License.

helicopter — An aircraft with large blades and no wings.

monoplane — An aircraft with a single set of wings.

navigator — The person responsible for making sure the aircraft stays on its course, successfully reaching its target and returning safely to base.

pilot — The person who flies, steers, and commands the aircraft.

pilot in command — The person in the aircraft who is responsible for its safe operation during the flight.

prisoner of war — Any person who is captured by the enemy during or immediately after an armed conflict, such as war.

recruitment The process of selecting people to train for military service.

squadron A group of military aircraft that form a section of the air force.

stopover When a fight leaves its original takeoff location and stops overnight or longer in another location before it arrives at its final destination. By comparison, a *layover* is a shorter stop, usually less than four hours.

turbulence When movement in the air, from weather or other conditions, causes motion on the plane.

REFERENCES

Atlantic Canada Aviation Museum. "Flight Simulators." acamuseum.ca/on-display/flight-simulators

———. "Our History." acamuseum.ca/the-museum/our-history/

Bates, Jim, and O'Malley, Dave, with Major Mathias Joost and Terry Higgins. "Flying Officer Allan Bundy: The RCAF's First Black Pilot." Vintage Wings of Canada, republished by Government of Canada: National Defence. February 26, 2016. canada.ca/en/department-national-defence/maple-leaf/rcaf/migration/2016/flying-officer-allan-bundy-the-rcaf-s-first-black-pilot.html

Black Cultural Centre for Nova Scotia. "Black Battalion." bccns.com/our-history/black-battalion-history

Blake, Emily. "'Freddie the Flyer' chronicles exploits of the North's first Indigenous pilo." The Canadian Press, July 19, 2023. thestar.com/entertainment/books/freddie-the-flyer-chronicles-exploits-of-the-north-s-first-indigenous-pilot/article_6c3a596a-c86a-50cb-bf62-b24508b241a3.html

Byard, Matthew. "Ardel Smith's Career as a Helicopter Pilot Takes Him to Great Heights." *Halifax Examiner*. June 6, 2022. .halifaxexaminer.ca/black-nova-scotia/ardel-smiths-career-as-a-helicopter-pilot-takes-him-to-great-heights

The Canadian Encyclopedia. "Allan Bundy." n.d. thecanadianencyclopedia.ca/en/article/allan-bundy

Canada's Aviation Hall of Fame. "Elizabeth Muriel Gregory MacGill." January 27, 2021. cahf.ca/elizabeth-muriel-gregory-macgill

CBC News. "90 years after her transatlantic flight, Amelia Earhart celebrated as trailblazer." cbc.ca/news/canada/newfoundland-labradoramelia-earhart-harbour-grace-90th-anniversary-1.6460910

———. "Frederick James Carmichael." October 24, 2020. cahf.ca/frederick-james-carmichael

———. "Longtime Friends Make Company History as Cougar Helicopters' 1st All-Female Flight Crew." June 18, 2021.cbc.ca/news/canada/newfoundland-labrador/rumbolt-helicopter-female-pilot-1.6066776

Cooke, Alex. "George Borden, Champion of Black Canadian Military History, Has Died." CBC News. December 4, 2020. cbc.ca/news/canada/nova-scotia/george-borden-champion-black-canadian-military-history-1.5827022

CTV News. "First Female Pilot from Opaskwayak Cree Nation Inspiring Others." Winnipeg, MB. August 26, 2022. winnipeg.ctvnews.ca/first-female-pilot-from-opaskwayak-cree-nation-inspiring-others-1.6044484

CTV Winnipeg. "Pilots Take Flight as Manitoba's First Female Indigenous Medevac Team." March 9, 2018. winnipeg.ctvnews.ca/pilots-take-flight-as-manitoba-s-first-female-indigenous-medevac-team-1.3835297? cache=%3FautoPlay%3Dtrue%3FclipId%3D1745623%3Fcontact-Form%3Dtrue

Government of Canada. "No. 2 Construction Battalion." June 29, 2021. canada.ca/en/army/services/events/2-construction-battalion.html

Lockheed Martin. "The S-92® Helicopter." December 14, 2022. lockheedmartin.com/en-us/products/sikorsky-s-92-helicopter.html

Metcalfe-Chenail, Danielle, and Fred Carmichael. *Freddie the Flyer*. Toronto, ON: Tundra Books, 2023.

Ninety-nines Canada. n.d. "Eileen Vollick." canadian99s.com/eileen-vollick-2/

Oyeniran, Channon. "Sleeping Car Porters in Canada." The Canadian Encyclopedia. February 8, 2019.thecanadianencyclopedia.ca/en/article/sleeping-car-porters-in-canada

Parks Canada Agency, Government of Canada. "First Aeroplane Flying in Canada — National Historic Event." March 7, 2022. parks.canada.ca/culture/designation/evenement-event/premier-vol-first-flying

Petruzzello, Melissa. "Amelia Earhart." *Encyclopædia Britannica*. britannica.com/biography/Amelia-Earhart

Royal Airforce Museum. "Supermarine Spitfire Vb." Wales, UK, 2020. rafmuseum.org.uk/research/collections/supermarine-spitfire-vb/

Royal Canadian Air Force "J.A.D. McCurdy: The Father of Canadian Military Aviation," March 29, 2019. canada.ca/en/department-national-defence/maple-leaf/rcaf/2019/04/j-a-d-mccurdy-the-father-of-canadian-military-aviation.html

———. "Junius Lyman Edward Hokan: An Extraordinary RCAF Officer." February 17, 2021. canada.ca/en/department-national-defence/maple-leaf/rcaf/2021/02/junius-lyman-edward-hokan-an-extraordinary-rcaf-officer.html

Sarty, Roger, and Dundas, Barbara. "Women in the Canadian Armed Forces." The Canadian Encyclopedia. February 7, 2006. thecanadianencyclopedia.ca/en/article/women-in-the-military

Verdict Media Limited. "Medium-Lift Multi-Role Twin-Engine Helicopter, Sikorsky S-92." Aerospace-Technology.com. 2017. aerospace-technology.com/projects/s92

Veterans Affairs Canada. "The Carty Brothers." February 26, 2020. veterans.gc.ca/en/remembrance/people-and-stories/carty-brothers

———. "Wars and Conflicts — Veterans Affairs Canada." January 23, 2020. veterans.gc.ca/en/remembrance/wars-and-conflicts

———. "James Moses." n.d. greatwaralbum.ca/Great-War-Album/About-the-Great-War/Air-Force/James-Moses

Vintage Wings of Canada. "Black Buffalo." vintagewings.ca/stories/black-buffalo

Wartime Canada. "114th Battalion CEF." Accessed October 5, 2024. wartimecanada.ca/document/first-world-war/contemporary-accounts/114th-battalion-cef

IMAGE CREDITS

The publisher has made all possible attempts to locate copyright holders for images.

Alamy: p. 60 | Allison Rumbolt: p. 64, p. 65 | Author's collection : p. 17; p. 19; pp. 72–73 | Black Cultural Centre for Nova Scotia: p. 15 | © Canada Post: p. 16 | Canadian Aviation Hall of Fame: p. 58 | Canadian War Museum: p. 33. Credit: CWM 20100197-001_64b, No. 14 Service Flying Training School, Aylmer, Ontario | DND Archives: p. 12; p. 32 | Fred Carmichael: pp. 45–46 | © His Majesty The King in Right of Canada represented by the OSGG. Reproduced with the permission of Office of the Secretary to the Governor General, 2024: p. 63 | iStock: p. 20; p. 55 | Jennifer Gawor: p. 61 | John Moses: p. 43; p. 44 (top) | Kim Ballantyne: pp. 47–49 | Library Archives Canada: p. 18 (PA-137188); p. 21 (PA-065157); p. 27 (R12294-960-1-E); p. 59 (3222847) | Mohamed Samanter: p. 68 | Nova Scotia Archives: p. 13 | Pexels : p. 1; p. 5; p. 9 (top); p. 37 | Province of Nova Scotia: p. 70–71 | Raven Beardy: p. 50, pp. 53–55 | RCAF: p. 8 (top); p. 24 (top & bottom); p. 36; p. 39 | 404 Squadron Archives: p. 25; p. 30 | Robyn Shlachetka: pp. 50–52 | Santiago Arias Camacho: p. 8 (bottom) | Shutterstock: p. 6; p. 9 (bottom); p. 23; p. 62 (bottom); p. 65 | Veterans Affairs Canada: p. 35; p. 41 | Vintage Wings of Canada (Windsor Communities, Windsor Mosaic): p. 28 | Wikimedia Commons: p. 31; p. 62 (top)

INDEX

Numerals in **bold** refer to aircraft. Numerals in *italics* refer to images.

Symbols

14th Battery, 4th Brigade 35
57th Squadron of the Royal Flying Corps 44
107th Infantry Battalion 44
401 Squadron 39, 40
404 (Buffalo) Squadron *30*, 32
410 Squadron 63
747 (jet) 6

A

Aerial Experiment Association 13
Airbus A330 72, 73
Airbus H135 8
Air Cadet League of Canada 22, 61
Air Care 53
Aklavik/Fred Carmichael Airport 47
Atlantic Canada Aviation Museum 74–75
ATR 42 55
aviation maintenance technician 63

B

B-17 Flying Fortress bomber *39*, 40
Baldwin, Casey 13
Ballantyne, Kimberly 10, *47*, 48, *49*
Barker, William 12
Battle of Britain 37, 60
Beardy, Raven 50, 51, *52*, *53*, 55, *54*
Bell, Alexander Graham 13
Bellanca Aircruiser 77
Bell, Gerald 28
Bishop, Billy 11, 12
Bjornson, Rosella 58
Black Battalion. *see* No. 2 Construction Battalion
Black Cultural Centre for Nova Scotia 17
Blériot XI Scarabée 76
Bollen, Ella Grace 35
Borden, Curtiss *17*
Borden, George *17*
Borden, Ozell *17*
Borden, Wilfred *17*
Bristol Beaufighter *31*
British Commonwealth Air Training Plan (BCATP) 20, 76, 77
British Royal Flying Corps (RFC) 11, 12
British Royal Naval Air Service (RNAS) 11
Bundy, Allan Selwyn 10, *25*, 26, 27, 28, 29, *30*, 31, *33*, 34, 35
Bundy, Carl 33
Bundy, Milton 33
Bundy, Private William 25, 26, 33
Bundy, Ruth 25, 26
Burgess Dunne floatplane *12*, 76

C

C-90B King Air 9
Camm, Sir Sydney 59
Canada Aviation and Space Museum 75
Canadair CF-5 Freedom Fighter 74
Canadian Armed Forces 11, 23
Canadian Aviation Corps (CAC) 11, 12
Canadian Aviation Hall of Fame 45, 47, 60
Canadian Forces Snowbirds 22, *23*
Canadian Museum of Flight 75
Canadian Women's Auxiliary Air Force 22
Carmichael, Frederick James "Fred" 10, *45*, *46*
Carty, Albert 18
Carty Brothers 18, *19*
CC-130H Hercules 24
Cessna 172 5, 6
Cessna 180 55
CF-18 Hornet *20*, 21
CH-139 Jet Ranger 8
commercial pilot/pilot's license 5, 8, 9, 49, 50, 54, 79, 80
Commonwealth Air Training Plan Museum 21
Cougar Helicopters 65
Crane, Flora and Malcolm 48
CT-114 Tutor 22
CT-156 Harvard II 8, 9

The Sky's the Limit!

D

Dalhousie University 26
de Havilland DH82C Tiger Moth 77
De Havilland Mosquito 32
de Lesseps, Count Jacques 76
Department of National Defence 25
DH-4 *44*
Diamond DA20 Katana 60, *62*
Dieppe Raid 38–39
disabilities, pilots with 4, 7, 61, 62

E

Earhart, Amelia 57
Eastern Ontario Regiment 15
Elliott Air Service *57*
Engineering Institute of Canada 60

F

Fairchild Aircraft Limited 59
Federal Aviation Administration 78
First World War 11, 12, 14, 19, 33, 34, 43, 56
Fisher, Sergeant Alisha *63*, 64
flight simulators 77, 78
Focke-Wulf Fw-190 (Würger) 38
Four Seasons 70
Freedom Fighters 75
Freeman, Pilot Officer Tarrance 28

G

Gawor, Jennifer 60, *61*, 62
Government Civil Aviation Examination 57
Gwich'in First Nations 10, 45

H

Halifax Stanfield International Airport 74
Handley Page Hampden 75
Hawker Hurricanes 59, 60
Hercules 54
Hercules CC130 76

Hodson, Squadron Leader Keith 39
Hokan, Junius Lyman Edward 10, *35*, *36*, 37, 38, 39, 40, *41*
Hokan, Kauri Lyman 35

I

International Space Station 75

J

Johnson, J. E. "Johnnie" 37
June Bug 13
Junkers Ju-88 bomber 38

K

Kane, Marie Della 26
King Air 53
King Air C-90B 8

L

Langley Regional Airport 75

M

MacGill, Elizabeth "Elsie" Muriel Gregory 59
McCurdy, Arthur 13
McCurdy, John Alexander Douglas 13
medevac 50–52, 55
Metcalfe-Chenail, Danielle 45, *46*, 47
Miller, Loretta 56
Missinippi Airways 48, 53
Montreal Aviation Museum 76
Moses, Lieutenant James David *43*, 44
Multi-Engine Training 8, 54

N

National Air Force Museum of Canada 76
National Search and Rescue Program of Canada 23
Navajo PA31 *52*
Ninety-Nines *49*, 57
No. 2 Construction Battalion *15*, 16, 18, 25, 33

Index 87

No. 6 RCAF Dunnville Museum 76
No. 18 Air Cadet Squadron 33
No. 56 Operational Training Unit 37
No. 133 Squadron 40
No. 610 Squadron 37

O

Oakes, Jill 49
Opaskwayak Cree Nation 47
Ottawa Flying Club 68
Otti, Eden 73

P

Payette, HRH Julie 63
Pimicikamak First Nation 51
Piper Archer 5, *6*
Piper Warrior PA-28 55
Porter Airlines 73
private pilot/ pilot licence 5, 49, 52, 60, 79

R

Royal Air Force (RAF) 31, 37
Ramsden, Herbert "Bert" 32
RCAF 6, 7, 8, 10, 11, 12, 19, 20, 21, 23, 24, 26, 28, 29, 35, 38, 40, 56, 59, 63, 67, 69
RCAF badge *24*
RCAF pilot wings *8*, 29, 37
RCAF Women's Division 21, 22
RCMP 27
recreational pilot certificate 79
Red Wing 13
Reid, Daniel 72, *73*
Rotary Wing Training 8
Royal Aviation Museum of Western Canada 77
Royal Canadian Legion 34
Royal Engineers 25
Ruck, Senator Calvin 16
Ruiz-Stonge, Tiffany *73*
Rumbolt, Captain Allison 65, *64*

S

Samanter, Captain Mohamed 67, *68*, 69, *73*
Saskatchewan Aviation Museum 77
Saskatoon International Airport 77
Savard, Roger "Roj" 32
Schweizer SGS 2-33 60, *62*
search-and-rescue 32, 40, 46, 54
Second World War 18, 19, 21, 30, 31, 34, 38, 41, 56, 59, 60, 75, 76, 77
Shamattawa First Nation 50, 53, 54
Shlachetka, Robyn 50, *51*, 55
Sikorsky S-92 *65*
Silver Dart 13
Six Nations of the Grand River reserve 43
Smith, Ardel 69, *70*, *71*
Spitfire Mk Vb *37*, 38
student pilot license 79

T

The Pas Airport 48
Transair 58
Trollip, Douglas 44

U

United States Air Force 23

V

Vollick, Eileen 56, *57*

W

Wabowden 50
Walker, Wilhelmina 22
Watts, E. V. 28
Webb, First Officer Zoe *64*
White Wing 13
Wright, Flight Sergeant Harry Elwood 30

The Sky's the Limit!